Be a
Conqueror!

A Practical Guide to Walking in Freedom and Victory

Silvia Sauve

Foreword by Doris M. Wagner

This book is published in Spanish as:
!Sé más que Vencedor!

Dedication

To all the brave and courageous men and women who dare to say to the darkness: NO MORE!

You can no longer mess with my life!
You can no longer touch my finances or my family!
You can no longer obstruct the destiny God has
for me!
I'll have no more of you!

To all those brave and courageous people who have decided to fight for their destiny.

I am certain that God is with you:

"So be strong and courageous! Do not be afraid and do not panic before them. For the LORD your God will personally go ahead of you. He will neither fail you nor abandon you." Deuteronomy 31:6

I am certain that God will honor your efforts:

"….I will honor those who honor me." 1 Samuel 2:30

I am certain that you will prosper:

> *"Be strong and very courageous. Be careful to obey all the instructions Moses gave you. Do not deviate from them, turning either to the right or to the left. Then you will be successful in everything you do."* Joshua 1:7

Again, I invite you to be strong and very brave!

Now, let's discover how to live with abundant blessings, fulfilling God's purpose for our lives.

Contents

Foreword

DORIS M. WAGNER

I thoroughly enjoyed reading this compact, practical, training manual. I wish I had a little book like this when I was a new believer nearly 70 years ago! It truly is a "Practical Guide To Walking in Freedom and Victory." I found this book very easy to read and especially agreed with all of the sound, biblical teaching, and enjoyed the supporting Scripture references throughout. I highly recommend it be translated into multiple foreign languages and strewn all over the world for new converts to gain a strong footing in their newfound faith and freedom.

I particularly enjoyed the chapter on giving. I used to teach "Stewardship" to all our new member classes in a large church in California. My deceased husband Peter, and I loved to give, and taught on the "graduated tithe." We taught that you start with what is God's, the ten percent. In this book, Silvia underlines the fact that the 10% is on gross earnings, not take-home pay. We thoroughly agree. God comes first, then the government gets its cut! Then you increase by percentage, little by little, albeit steadily, and watch and see what God does. These are your offerings. The tithe belongs to God. As a matter of fact, when we made our paycheck deposits, we opened a separate account for our giving so that funds would never be co-mingled. It made for easier bookkeeping and we were never tempted to use God's money for a personal need or desire. For example, when a special need from a missionary came to light, I would ask Peter: "How much money has God got?" We always knew the exact amount. We might be able to give a generous gift to a special project. We were big believers in supporting our home church first, since that is where we are fed with God's Word. I believe that generous giving can be a special spiritual gift but I also firmly believe that God sees to it that our needs are met and overflowing when we give the first and best generous gifts we can to Him.

Another fun chapter asks the reader to take a good look at what is in the home. Spiritual housecleaning is a neglected subject and there may be openings there that Satan can use to torment the occupants.

Every other chapter is vital to healthy spiritual growth for a new convert or newly delivered person. Old-timers in the faith will greatly be encouraged as many other spiritual guidelines are thoroughly examined in a practical, concise and soundly biblical manner. Silvia does not waste words. I highly recommend this for small group Bible study. Each short chapter is pure meat, delicious and nourishing.

Doris M. Wagner
Minister at Glory of Zion and Global Spheres Center
Denton, Texas
May 2018

Preface

DR. WILLIAM SUDDUTH

Over the last 12 years I have watched the Lord take Silvia to become a vibrant woman of God. She is a great teacher who has a passion to see the people of God walk in freedom and to become all they have been created to be in His plan. Silvia has a tremendous desire to communicate with depth and clarity the biblical principles for deliverance and lasting freedom. Because of her dedication and study, I was very pleased a few years ago to appoint Silvia and her husband Ernie the Hispanic Ambassadors for the International Society of Deliverance Ministers.

I personally have seen an upswing of interest in the ministry of deliverance and inner healing recently. I recommend this book as an important contribution and necessary reading for all who have recently gone through the process of deliverance and for new converts. The principles outlined in her book: *Be More Than a Conqueror: A Practical Guide to Walk in Freedom and Victory* will be a great help to maintain personal freedom and establish a firm foundation for the fulfillment of God's plan in your life.

Dr. Bill Sudduth
Presiding Apostle and President
International Society of Deliverance Ministers
Righteous Acts Ministries

Acknowledgments

I give infinite thanks to God for helping me discover what is written about me in the books of heaven according to Psalm 139:16. I remember very vividly the early days of having confessed Christ as Lord and Savior of my life; I had an insatiable hunger for His Word and would spend hours scrutinizing it and asking God to teach me. One particular day I was sitting alone in my living room doing my devotional, when suddenly I started to hear a strange noise, something I had never heard before. I quickly realized the sound was coming from the kitchen, and that the cutlery inside the kitchen drawer was making a loud noise. The silverware was bouncing around inside the drawer when "nobody" was moving anything! I was sure that it was Satan trying to induce fear in me and take back the territory in my life that I had taken from him. With this realization, I jumped up from the sofa, entered the kitchen, and with a newly discovered authority I ordered him to leave in the name of Jesus. I felt an incredible courage bubble up within me, and I had no fear. I told him that my house was Christ's and that he had no right to be there. To my surprise, the silverware stopped bouncing in the drawer immediately and it never happened again. God was revealing to me early on that He had called me to be an instrument in His hands to minister in the area of deliverance. Thank you, my Lord!

Thanks to Dr. Peter Wagner and Doris Wagner for their wonderful legacy; if it were not for them, this guide would not exist. I give thanks for your conviction that deliverance is a key piece for the advancement of the Kingdom of God. Dr. Peter is in heaven now, but I remember when I heard him say: "the language of heaven is Spanish." In truth he had a heart for Hispanic people. Mrs. Doris is with us still and very strong. I appreciate your dedication and your love to see people free from bondage. Thank you for praying for us and allowing us to take the baton in this relay race. I recently heard her say, "I'm getting excited to do personal deliverance again." Go ahead Mrs. Doris! God will continue to use you powerfully!

Deep thanks to Dr. Bill Sudduth for taking my husband and I under his care and mentorship. I equally thank you for having a heart for Hispanics, for thinking big and visualizing a Hispanic branch for the International Society of Deliverance Ministers (ISDM). Thank you for believing in us and naming us the Hispanic Ambassadors of ISDM (www.isdmministers.org/espanol). We trust that with God's help and our efforts, we will be able to carry out yours and Dr. Wagner's vision of having Deliverance teams in the churches.

Thanks to my husband, Dr. Ernest Sauve Jr., for tirelessly praying and fasting until we see our prophetic destiny as deliverance ministers unfold as we respond to our call before the Lord.

Thanks to our precious daughter that God has given us, for sowing faithfully into our ministry. Thank you for being a constant blessing so we can expand our territory and bless the nations.

I also thank all those in the family of the faith who in one way or another have helped us throughout the years. Thank you for your prayers, for your support and for your trust. Especially those who have received ministry and counseling from us, who play a decisive and very important role in the preparation of this manual.

Introduction

CONGRATULATIONS!

With all my heart and with great pleasure I want to congratulate you. If you have this book in your hands you have probably gone through the deliverance process or are seriously considering it. Since I went through this process myself (a long time ago), I have always believed that deliverance is for the brave. Not all dare to open their lives and bring to light situations from the past that have been painful or even shameful. The brave dare to let the light of Christ illuminate the darkness that dwells in their minds and hearts. Those who dare even experience physical health. It is proven that emotional wounds and spiritual oppression are often manifested in diseases, allergies and ailments that affect our body.

Once again congratulations! The fact that you have this book in your hands is an excellent indication that you are brave and have an outstanding disposition to face your traumas and fears. Your desire to confront the lies the enemy has told you (and that you may have believed) is admirable. It is time to replace all those lies with the truth that is the Word of God and His great love for you. You have gone through an arduous and painful road, but you have won!

I would love to be able to tell you that this is it, that after the deliverance process everything is good, that you will have no more problems and that from now on all will be wonderful and rosy. Unfortunately, I cannot – because I would be lying to you. God tells us in His Word:

> *"I have told you these things, so that in me you may have peace. In this world you will have trouble. But take heart! I have overcome the world."* John 16:33

God says that we will have troubles, we will have problems and difficult situations; it is not a matter of "probably," it is a matter of "surely." Without a doubt, throughout our lives we will have to face difficult situations. On the other hand, God tells us to have peace and trust in Him. God promises us afflictions, but at the same time He promises us victory over those afflictions as long as we walk in His word and trust in Him fully.

This is not to say that this reality presents us with good news and bad news. Indeed, this is all good news! This is because we know that we will be victorious whenever we do things God's way. That is why it is so important to know His ways, because without that knowledge we will be an easy prey for the enemy.

> *"My people are destroyed from lack of knowledge."*
> Hosea 4:6

We do not want to be destroyed because of lack of knowledge. So, in the next chapters, I invite you to discover

God's ways in order to maintain your freedom and walk in victory. Will you come with me?

Chapter 1

Why should I be on guard?

As mentioned in the introduction, it is false to think that after deliverance everything will be fine. You must be prepared and be on guard because the attacks will come. The enemy will always return and will try to take back the land that has been taken from him. God will always be with you, but you have a determining role to play in all of this. It is your responsibility to keep the doors closed so that the enemy does not enter. Not in vain does the Word of God say in Ephesians 4:27, *"give no place to the devil."* Here the word "place" comes from the original Greek "topos" which is the origin of the word "topography." "Place" is therefore: land, sector or part of your life.

Parts of your life can include your health, your finances, your family, etc. When the enemy is given a "place," in reality what you give him is a legal right so that he can attack in any of the areas that are most relevant to your life where you are most vulnerable.

During the reading of this practical guide we will discover how to keep the devil out of all the places that concern our life, because he will surely try to attack again.

You probably wonder if the devil will really try to attack you again. It is always good to remove doubts with the Word of God, because the Bible is true. With this in mind, we are going to look at the case of Jesus, when the Holy Spirit took him to the desert according to Luke 4:1-13

"Then Jesus, full of the Holy Spirit, returned from the Jordan River. He was led by the Spirit in the wilderness, where he was tempted by the devil for forty days. Jesus ate nothing all that time and became very hungry. Then the devil said to him, 'If you are the Son of God, tell this stone to become a loaf of bread.' But Jesus told him, 'No! The Scriptures say, "People do not live by bread alone."' Then the devil took him up and revealed to him all the kingdoms of the world in a moment of time. 'I will give you the glory of these kingdoms and authority over them,' the devil said, 'because they are mine to give to anyone I please. I will give it all to you if you will worship me.' Jesus replied, 'The Scriptures say, "You must worship the LORD your God and serve only him."' Then the devil took him to Jerusalem, to the highest point of the Temple, and said, 'If you are the Son of God, jump off! For the Scriptures say, "He will order his angels to protect and guard you. And they will hold you up with their hands so you won't even hurt your foot on a stone."' Jesus responded, 'The Scriptures also say, "You must not test the LORD your God."' When the devil had finished tempting Jesus, he left him until the next opportunity came.'

Notice that in Luke 4:2 it says that Jesus was tempted by the devil. As we continue reading, we see that he keeps trying three times, but Jesus always silences him with the Word saying, "it is written." Now look at Luke 4:13 *"When the devil had finished tempting Jesus, he left him until the next opportunity came."* Very clear, right? If it is *"until the next opportunity"* it means that he tried again.

Now, we know that the devil tried many times as per Hebrews 4:15: *"This High Priest of ours understands our weaknesses, for he faced all of the same testings we do, yet he did not sin."* **Jesus was tested in everything but He never sinned.**

Let me ask you something: if the enemy tempted Jesus again, and again, do you think he will not do so with us too? I can assure you that yes, he will! We must be prepared and, like Jesus, we need to silence the enemy with the Word. At the same time, we must keep the spiritual doors and windows in our lives tightly closed.

Let us see another example in the Bible that assures us that the enemy will return. This time the second attack is worse because several demons attack in unison. Matthew 12:43-45 reads:

> *"When an unclean spirit goes out of a man, he goes through dry places, seeking rest, and finds none. Then he says, 'I will return to my house from which I came.' And when he comes, he finds it empty, swept, and put in order. Then he goes and takes with him seven other spirits more wicked than himself, and they enter and dwell there; and the last state of that man is worse than the first"*

It is very clear that the unclean spirit made his home inside the man. Then it says that the unclean spirit comes out of man (referring to the human race, i.e., both men and women), but it seeks rest and cannot find it, so it decides to return to where it came from.

Here we can take a short break and reflect. Do you remember when the demons were being expelled from you? I remember when they were expelled from me. I remember the deliverance minister commanding the demon to leave in the name of Jesus. Sometimes the demon left without much struggle and very quickly. Other times it took longer, but in the end, they all came out. When all legal rights are removed, the demons have to leave – they have no more grounds to stay. I remember the peace I felt after all those evil forces were expelled.

I knew something had come out – I could not explain it very well with words, but my whole being felt different. Then I learned just as you now know, that one or more demons were evicted from their home – they were evicted from my body, from my mind, from my emotions; from wherever they were. We do know that they do not dwell in our spirit because the Holy Spirit dwells in our spirit since the time we accepted Christ as our Lord and Savior; but from wherever they were, they left.

Those demons that came out will come back; when they do, they better find the house swept, adorned and, most importantly, *occupied* with the Word of God and *filled* with the Holy Spirit. If this is not the case, we will be in serious trouble. It is crucial that your house (your whole being: your mind, your heart, your emotions) is not empty, but is instead filled with the Holy Spirit. That is why your daily reading of the Bible, your time of worship to the Lord and your time of intercession and speaking in tongues are so important. We will discover other important indications as we read this guide.

Chapter 2

The authority of the believer:

Your authority!

It is very important to know that when we pray and when we engage in spiritual warfare, we do it from a position of victory—not from a position of defeat. The Bible is clear and emphatic when it says that in Christ Jesus we are more than conquerors. We can see this in the book of Romans 8:37, *"Yet in all these things we are more than conquerors through Him who loved us."* A couple of verses before it talks about tribulation, anguish, persecution, hunger, danger, implying that Christ is above all these things, and that with Him and in Him, we are more than conquerors.

His Word says as well, in Ephesians 2:6 that we are sitting together with Christ in heaven. Ephesians 2:4-6 says *"But God, who is rich in mercy, because of His great love with which He loved us, even when we were dead in trespasses, made us alive together with Christ (by grace you have been saved), and raised us up together, and made us sit together in the heavenly places in Christ Jesus."*

I have to confess that many times my mind begins to ask me: how is it that we can be here on earth, but at the same time in heaven, together with Christ? I only say to my mind: it is written! If the Bible says it, I believe it! I do not walk by sight, but by faith! In addition, I command my thoughts to be submitted to the lordship of the Holy Spirit.

Truth is not what my mind says, nor what I feel; the truth is what is written.

The Word of God is true, and that is why it is so important to know it well. In the beginning you may start by silencing your mind from anything that comes against the word of God, but very soon your mind begins to be renewed and you start to think according to the Word.

I remember when I was a recently converted Christian, hearing many people in my church praying in this way: "Oh Lord, forgive my coming like this in front of you, because I am a filthy rag, a worm, I do not deserve…" I would listen to them and ask myself: what is their source of information? How do they get to those conclusions? My Bible said something different about my position, about my authority and therefore about my identity in Christ.

Since you and I are now a new creation, it means that it was before Christ that we were dead in our crimes and sins, but not now! Let's look at 2 Corinthians 5:17 *"Therefore, if anyone is in Christ, he is a new creation; old things have passed away; behold, all things have become new."*

I can assure you that now that you have gone through the deliverance process and all the legal rights have been taken away from the enemy, you can really operate from the reality that you are a new creature.

In his book "Unlocking Destinies from the Courts of Heaven" Robert Henderson[1] explains that although Christ has given us all blessings and authority, it is up to us to enforce what Christ has already given us by putting it into practice and making it a reality in our lives.

I will give you an example. Imagine that your uncle Peter has left you a fortune and that you now have to take a case of inheritance to the court. The judge rules in your favor, deciding that the inheritance is yours. Right at that moment the money is yours, but it is not in your bank account yet. The judge is not the one who takes the money out of uncle Peter's account and puts it into your account; the judge already did his job determining that the inheritance is really yours. The responsibility to move that money to your account is yours. You take the document the judge gave you to the bank where uncle Peter has the money, and that bank has to transfer the money into your account. If you do not do that chore you will never enjoy the money uncle Peter left for you.

The analogy here is that Jesus, like the judge in the example, already did His part: Jesus died on the cross for our sins and by His blood we are clean, we are a new creation, and we have abundant life. Now it is our responsibility to enforce and impose that truth in our lives, believing it and removing all legal rights the enemy has had to prevent us from operating from our position of victory that Jesus has given us.

You may have asked yourself why people who suffered from depression before they met Christ still suffer from depression after meeting Christ, or why people with fears or addictions still continue suffering with them; Aren't they a new creation? The answer is yes! Yes, they are a new creation, but they have not appropriated what belongs to them and they have not taken away the legal right from the enemy that they themselves or their ancestors gave him. Just as in the inheritance example: though they are millionaires and can buy a brand-new car, they are still walking or riding the bus.

This is very sad, but it is the truth for many Christians within the church. You have been brave, you went through deliverance and you took away the legal rights the enemy had over your life and your affairs. You took possession of the freedom Christ gave you on the cross and now you can really function as totally new in Christ.

Let's look at 1 Peter 2:9

"But you are a chosen generation, a royal priesthood, a holy nation, His own special people, that you may proclaim the praises of Him who called you out of darkness into His marvelous light"

Let's also look at Hebrews 10:19

"Therefore, brethren, having boldness to enter the Holiest by the blood of Jesus,"

How about that? Isn't that tremendous news? You are a chosen generation, a royal priesthood, a holy nation, His own special people (people acquired by God). Additionally, you have direct access to the presence of God, to the Holy of Holies because of the blood of Christ. So?

I do not know what you were before, but now you are important, blessed, and have delegated authority from the Lord!

Matthew 28:18 states: *"And Jesus came and spoke to them, saying, All authority has been given to me in heaven and on earth."*

Christ transferred that authority to His church. Christ ascended to heaven and is the head of the church, the church is the body. His authority has to be perpetuated through His body, which is you and me.[2] That is the reason why we are here on earth. In his book The Authority of the Believer, Kenneth E. Hagin says that we need to know what is ours, but knowing it is not enough. It is when we act on what we know what brings results.[3]

Remember: You have been brave going through the deliverance process. Now you can fully function as new creation in Christ with all His authority!

NOTES

1 Robert Henderson, Unlocking Destinies from the Courts of Heaven, p. 17.
2 Kenneth Hagin, The Authority of the Believer, Spanish version, 2002 p. 7
3 Kenneth Hagin, The Authority of the Believer, 1996 p. 14

Chapter 3

Is your house truly clean?

You probably answer: Of course! I swept the floor and wiped it with water and disinfectant; I even dusted all the furniture and everything is clean and smells very good. Let me congratulate you for that, but we are really talking about another type of cleaning. We are talking about the spiritual cleansing of both your house and the land where your house is located.

I remember when I did the spiritual cleansing of my apartment where I lived right after completing the deliverance process. I felt that my spiritual eyes had been opened and what had gone unnoticed before I could now see very clearly. I remember I had just arrived from a trip where I had bought many decorations for the apartment. I had visited several places with Chinese and Egyptian crafts that were my favorites at the time. Back then I did not know how terrible many of them are from the perspective of the spiritual realm. I had bought two dragons that looked like jade, each one about 10 inches high. These dragons were in a high place in the living room so I was able to see them as soon as I opened the front door. Additionally, I was able to see them as I walked across the living room towards the more private rooms like our bedrooms. For several days after having completed the deliverance process, I felt the dragons' eyes following me throughout the room; from the moment I opened the front door to well into the hallway that led to the bedrooms. I wanted to throw them away, but I kept thinking about how expensive they had been and that it would be a big waste to throw them out.

I had a similar feeling about some Egyptian jewelry I had bought. It was a precious set of earrings and a necklace—a replica of certain Egyptian's dynasty with many colors and carved stones. Every time I put on those jewels, I felt different. I was afraid and distrustful of everything and everyone. Like with the dragons, I did not want to throw them away because they were beautiful and very expensive.

I knew I had to throw them away, but my flesh did not want to. So, as I do very often, I went to the Bible to find out what God says about this and about what I (and we) should do.

You probably wonder why I should get rid of those things? And the answer is simple:

Because everything that does not glorify God brings darkness, death and defeat in our lives.

A very clear example is in Genesis 35:19 with the untimely death of Rachel. Let's look:

"So Rachel died and was buried on the way to Ephrath (that is, Bethlehem)"

Previously we see in Genesis 31:32-35 that Rachel lies to hide the idols that she had stolen from her father, Laban. Let's see:

> "'With whomever you find your gods, do not let him live. In the presence of our brethren, identify what I have of yours and take it with you.' For Jacob did not know that Rachel had stolen them. And Laban went into Jacob's tent, into Leah's tent, and into the two maids' tents, but he did not find them. Then he went out of Leah's tent and entered Rachel's tent. Now Rachel had taken the household idols, put them in the camel's saddle, and sat on them. And Laban searched all about the tent but did not find them. And she said to her father, 'Let it not displease my lord that I cannot rise before you, for the manner of women is with me.' And he searched but did not find the household idols"

So, we see that Rachel's disobedience resulted in her premature death.

We see a similar example in Joshua chapters 6 and 7 where Israel suffers an overwhelming defeat at the hands of a relatively small enemy after having a stunning victory against an extremely powerful enemy like Jericho.

God had given exact instructions to not take anything from the people of Jericho saying that if they did, they would bring problems and disastrous consequences on themselves. Let's see:

> "And you, by all means abstain from the accursed things, lest you become accursed when you take of the accursed

things, and make the camp of Israel a curse, and trouble it." Joshua 6:18

But Israel paid no attention:

"But Israel violated the instructions about the things set apart for the LORD. A man named Achan had stolen some of these dedicated things, so the LORD was very angry with the Israelites. Achan was the son of Carmi, a descendant of Zimri son of Zerah, of the tribe of Judah." Joshua 7:1

As a result of this, Israel was defeated:

"So approximately 3,000 warriors were sent, but they were soundly defeated. The men of Ai chased the Israelites from the town gate as far as the quarries, and they killed about thirty-six who were retreating down the slope. The Israelites were paralyzed with fear at this turn of events, and their courage melted away." Joshua 7:4-5

Joshua did not know what had happened—he was not aware that one of his men had disregarded the order that God had given. God explains it to Joshua in this way:

"Israel has sinned and broken my covenant! They have stolen some of the things that I commanded must be set apart for me. And they have not only stolen them but have lied about it and hidden the things among their own belongings. That is why the Israelites are running from their enemies in defeat. For now Israel itself has been set

apart for destruction. I will not remain with you any longer unless you destroy the things among you that were set apart for destruction." Joshua 7:11-12

It is very serious to have things in our possession that do not glorify God, worse yet, to possess things that He detests.

If we want God's protection over our lives we must destroy everything He does not approve of.

I will share a list of objects that do not glorify God[1]

1. Foreign Gods
2. False Religions
3. Occult Objects
4. Secret-Society Objects
5. Other Objects

FOREIGN GODS

This list is related to what God says in the book of Exodus.

"You must not make for yourself an idol of any kind or an image of anything in the heavens or on the earth or in the sea. You must not bow down to them or worship them, for I, the LORD your God, am a jealous God who will not tolerate your affection for any other gods. I lay the sins of the parents upon their children; the entire

family is affected—even children in the third and fourth generations of those who reject me." Exodus 20:4-5

I must confess that when I read this in the Scriptures for the first time I felt very bad because I discovered that I had been taught quite differently in the school where I studied as a child. My family did not spend much time at church, but every once in a while, we would go to a Catholic church. I remember that my dad did not miss a Resurrection Sunday. My three sisters and I studied in Catholic schools where the nuns were very demanding; you had to follow their orders or there would be serious consequences. Those who have studied with Catholic nuns in Latin America know what I am talking about. We had to follow their guidelines and worship many idols: all of the so-called "virgins" (Mary, Fatima, Guadalupe, etc.) and all of the so-called "saints" (Joseph, Peter, Francis, etc.). We had to light candles to all of those idols and get on our knees before them. I have always asked myself: Do they not have the book of Exodus in their Bibles? Could it be that they have not read it? Or did they simply decide to ignore it?

Not only are these idols within many Catholic churches and schools, but also in homes and backyards. It is very common to see small shrines with those idols where people worship by bringing flowers, lighting candles, kneeling before them, etc. I used to do that. I give glory to God for opening my eyes to what His word says instead.

This is not the only example of foreign gods. There are also the Buddhas, the famous Egyptian pyramids, the elephants with the raised trunk and all the new-age objects including Chinese metaphysics such as Feng Shui and others. People place these "gods" in their homes in the hopes of attracting "abundance and prosperity." Let me tell you that all that is being attracted is the abundance of problems. All these "gods" must be removed from our homes.

Images and religious relics, in the form of earrings, rings, pictures, or ornaments that represent some form of idol, also displease God. Images of virgins, saints, zodiac signs, and even new era's images like the sun and the moon, that many people idolize, also must be removed from our homes.

When you are making an inventory of what is inside your house you should always ask yourself: What is the origin of that object? What is the purpose of that object? Does that object glorify God? When traveling, be very careful with what you buy and bring into your home as an ornament. Always ask the Holy Spirit and He will guide you.

FALSE RELIGIONS

Remember that God detests when we put our trust in other things, since we should trust in Him alone. God does not want us to participate in any other religion, nor does He wants us to place our trust in any object, nor in ourselves, nor in own our minds.

Everyone is familiar with the diversity of religions such as Buddhism, Islam, Hinduism, Catholicism, Mormonism, Jehovah's Witnesses, Rosicrucianism and many others. People are also familiar with relaxation methods like Yoga, the Silva mind control, and other methods for so-called "transcendental meditation." We must find all the books, magazines, manuals and "prayers" or mantras related with those religions (or relaxation methods) that may be inside our homes and destroy them.

Beware if you have visited a pagan temple and bought something there that you now have at home. Without giving it a second thought, please destroy it and remove it from your home.

OCCULT OBJECTS

The list of these objects can be very long, but we will name some, trusting that you will ask the Holy Spirit to guide you to complete the rest of your list. Objects related with horoscope, astrology, tarot cards, any occult game such as the Ouija board and demonic cards. Any object considered "good luck," "good charm," "protective amulet," "to attract prosperity" like the famous plates filled with rice and coins, and even plants considered for that purpose. Any object used to predict the future such as cards, crystal balls, pendulums and other crystals. Any object or instrument for witchcraft, Santeria, white magic, black magic, for adoration of demons, or used to practice Satanism, like potions, voodoo dolls and others. Any object of the new era like angels, colored candles according to the day of the week, and aromatic incense for relaxation and to clear the mind.

All these objects must be destroyed without contemplation and regardless of the financial value they may have. The Scripture gives us a powerful example of this in the book of Acts 19:18-19:

"Many who became believers confessed their sinful practices. A number of them who had been practicing sorcery brought their incantation books and burned them at a public bonfire. The value of the books was several million dollars"

Can you imagine?

These new believers, after their eyes were opened, burned all the occult objects that were in their homes despite of what they paid for them.

We must do the same!

SECRET-SOCIETY OBJECTS

It was not until a few years ago that, while talking to my mother, I discovered that my grandfather had been a 32nd degree mason. I did not know much about him because he died when my mother was only fifteen years old. I personally think that he, like Rachel in Genesis 35:19, caused his own premature death because of sinful practices detestable to the Lord.

I also understood why so many people in my family suffer from allergies and respiratory problems. What happens is that the freemasons from their initiation up to when they reach higher degrees (such as the 32nd degree), often require their members to take oaths and go through initiation rituals, including pledging allegiance to various deities, which are completely contrary to God's Word.

Members curse themselves making vows against various parts of their body including the respiratory system. We should not be surprised then when we see so many people suffering with these illnesses, given that Freemasonry is very common in the entire world. In many cities and even in small towns, we see masonic lodges where masons gather to carry out their diabolical meetings.

I highly recommend all people, whose ancestors have been involved in Freemasonry, to do the prayer of renunciation of "Breaking Masonic Curses."[2] This prayer will take the legal rights from the enemy and therefore remove the curses from over their lives.

There are countless secret societies; I will name only a few of them: Freemasonry, Shriners, Easter Star, Job's Daughters, Odd Fellows, Elks, Amaranth, DeMolay, Rainbow for Girls or Daughters of the Nile, fraternities (Kappa Sigma, Lambda Chi Alpha, Phi Delta Theta, etc.), and sororities. The way they convince people, and especially young people in universities, to join them is by making them believe that belonging to one of these secret societies will facilitate their professional advancement and will give them prestige. What people do not know is that they are practically selling their soul to the devil in exchange for social status and short-lived financial gain. The devil will let them enjoy those pleasures for a very short time, but he will charge for those favors more than they can ever repay. They may experience good social status but they will not have peace in their hearts and, like my grandfather, will most likely die prematurely.

"For the wages of sin is death…" Romans 6:23

Throughout the course of ceremonies that take place in these secret societies, people often acquire paraphernalia such as rings, books, clothes, etc. Members are often encouraged to carry these objects with them, and may even be passed down from generation to generation. It is very important that you check what you have in your home, especially the "memory trunk" that is sitting in some storage space and that you may not have opened for years, and destroy everything related to objects connected to secret societies.

OTHER OBJECTS

Other things can also attract demonic activity to our homes; for example, elements of a sensual, sexual, violent, immoral, or illegal nature. You should look at the type of movies, magazines, books, music, video games, etc. in your house. What kind of games for both adults and children are in your home? Where do you go on the Internet? Are there drugs in your house? What kind of art is in your house? Is it the type of art that invites sensuality, nostalgia or depression?

You need to examine your customs, your culture and traditions, your type of entertainment, and ask yourself, "does each glorify God?" If the answer is "no," then you must get rid of it. Ask God for wisdom and He will give it to you.

Perhaps your mind is already thinking about different things you could have in your home. You probably did not know about them, but now you do. There was a time when I did not know either, but once I knew it, I made the decision to get rid of those things because I knew that they displeased God; moreover, they would bring curses to my life and my loved ones. Additionally, from a personal point of view, they were disturbing and bothering me. Surely the same thing is happening to you, particularly after having gone through the deliverance process. Very often your "spiritual" senses (i.e., your discernment) is more acute; now you can discern in the spirit with more certainty.

I remember that when I made the decision to remove all those objects from my residence, I called a sister from the church who was very connected with the deliverance ministers there. I told her what I wanted to do. She told me she would come to help me carry out the spiritual cleansing of my apartment. She came and the apartment ended up being practically empty. We took down all the strange wall paintings, we destroyed all the horror and violent movies, the magazines and worldly books, the gifts from past romantic relationships, weird dolls, and all new age ornaments including elephants, "prosperity plants," pyramids, and definitely the Egyptian jewels and Chinese dragons.

This is a delicate process and I recommend doing it with a mature believer who has understanding about (and some experience with) deliverance, as there may be demonic manifestations in the home throughout this process. These need to be addressed with wisdom and direction from the Holy Spirit. I specially recommend this for the first major spiritual cleansing of your home, as other routine cleanings can be done by yourself. Additionally, my recommendation is to burn or destroy all the items you are getting rid of. Under no circumstances should you sell or give those items away. Please remember that if those things bring curses to your life, they will also bring curses to other peoples' lives.

Sometimes, when the objects have been dedicated to high ranking evil entities, you may not be able to break them. That was the case with the Chinese dragons I mentioned before; even though we hit them with an iron hammer, they did not break. Thankfully I lived near the ocean and was able to throw them there; I hope no one finds them.

There are also spiritual portals that may not be connected with objects; rather, they can be connected to past actions carried out in specific locations. For example, there may be demonic activity in the land where a house is located, or in any of the rooms inside due to evil or demonic activity that may have taken place there. It is possible that the previous owners practiced witchcraft, or that they got into heated arguments and cursed each other. Perhaps there was physical abuse towards children or between spouses. Maybe the previous tenants could not afford the mortgage and were expelled, cursing the house and future owners in their departure. Many situations may have happened that you are not aware of.

I remember when my husband and I bought the house we currently live in—we began to hear noises inside the walls, as if a crazy man were trapped inside. The banging from within the walls was very strong, making it sound as if someone were trying to get out. We didn't know much about the history of the house; all we knew was that it had been built many years ago, that it had gone through many renovations and that it had passed through many different hands throughout the years.

By circumstances orchestrated by the Holy Spirit we found knives, chains and other strange objects buried underground in the patio. We prayed in all areas of the house and repented and asked God for forgiveness for all the sins committed in the house as the Holy Spirit was revealing. We also cast out all those unclean spirits that had remained stuck to the house as a result of the legal rights granted by the previous owners. Finally, we blessed each area of the house and anointed it with oil. I tell you, the noises stopped! Never again did we hear noises in the walls and everyone who enters our home says they feel peace there.

My husband and I greatly enjoy hosting pastors and ministers in our home. God has given us the gift of hospitality and we have had the privilege of hosting people who have been a tremendous blessing to our lives. I remember once we hosted a pastor from Venezuela who told us laughing, "Silvia, the only problem in your house is the silence, it is incredibly quiet here." He, like others, can feel the peace in our home.

My husband and I are very careful with what we bring into our home. During our trips we pay special attention to what we buy and what it is gifted to us. If the Holy Spirit says "don't take it inside your home," we take it seriously and we throw it away regardless of how beautiful or expensive the gift may have been.

We have decided that it is better to decorate our house with the Word of God.

"Listen, O Israel! The LORD is our God, the LORD alone. And you must love the LORD your God with all your heart, all your soul, and all your strength. And you must commit yourselves wholeheartedly to these commands that I am giving you today. Repeat them again and again to your children. Talk about them when you are at home and when you are on the road, when you are going to bed and when you are getting up. Tie them to your hands and wear them on your forehead as reminders. Write them on the doorposts of your house and on your gates."
Deuteronomy 6:4-9

We have ornaments and posters with the Word of God around the house. These days it is very easy to find them at the Christian bookstores and online; you have plenty of options to decorate your home in a way that glorifies the Lord, and it is a constant reminder of His word for the whole family.

I highly recommend Chuck D. Pierce's book: Protecting Your Home from Spiritual Darkness.[1] Dr. Pierce describes his book as follows: "Close the door to the enemy and open the door to God. Learn how to rid your home of destructive objects and spiritual darkness to create a fortress of love and light for your family. Too many Christians are completely unaware of how the enemy has gained access to their homes through what they own. This practical, easy-to-read book shows you how to pray through your home and property in order to lock out evil and experience a richer spiritual life."

I can assure you that if you follow the instructions in Chuck's book to clean and protect your home from spiritual darkness, you will enjoy the same peace we experience in ours. You can also visit our web page www.daystream.org and write to us. We'll be glad help you.

NOTES

1 Chuck D. Pierce & Rebecca Wagner Sytsema, Protecting Your Home From Spiritual Darkness, p. 33-35.
2 Dr. William Sudduth, Deliverance Training Manual, p. 37-44.

Chapter 4

What is the condition
of your mind?

What is the condition of your mind? This is not in reference to how smart you are, or how good your memory is, nor is it about whether you went to college and graduated "summa cum laude" or "almost not laude." In fact, this question has nothing to do with intelligence or intellectuality. It is about whether your mind is being renewed by the word of God; this will dictate your thought life and will guide your actions.

The Word of God is very clear when it talks about our way of thinking. It warns us that we should not think in the same way that the world thinks, but that on the contrary, we should let God change us with His word. Let's take a look:

> "Do not copy the behavior and customs of this world, but let God transform you into a new person by changing the way you think. Then you will learn to know God's will for you, which is good and pleasing and perfect."
> Romans 12:2

Now let's see: *"For as he thinks in his heart, so is he."* Proverbs 23:7

Your thoughts determine your lifestyle.

Imagine that there are two types of lenses. One type is that of the word of God, and the other type is that of all the other sources—family, friends, the media, and even your own intellect or education. The lens you choose will determine your vision of life; therefore, I can guarantee you that if your lens is the former, then your walk in this life will be guided by what God says.

Your thoughts determine your actions, and your actions determine your day-to-day and therefore your future.

Your thoughts impact absolutely everything around you: your family, your friends, your work, your business, your finances, etc. As such, we must make a constant effort to let God change our way of thinking and let His words be the lens through which we see.

Practical ways to change your thoughts:

- Renew your mind by reading the Bible daily
- Practice praise and worship continuously

- Decide to make God the Lord of all areas of your life
- Decide to purposely walk in holiness
- Watch your thoughts passionately

RENEW YOUR MIND BY READING THE BIBLE DAILY

You can start with the New Testament from Matthew to Revelation, and later you can read the whole Bible starting from the Old Testament onwards. Many people read the entire Bible in a year, but do not worry about that. I once heard someone say that the important thing was not how fast you go through the entire Scripture (Bible), but how fast the Scripture goes through you. The important thing is that the words written in the Bible be written in you, your way of thinking and your way of life. Try to read at least one complete chapter daily, and have a notebook where you write down what you feel the Lord is teaching you or asking you to do.

Sometimes during my daily reading, the Lord asks me to fast for a certain period of time, or to pray for a specific person, or to send that person a word of encouragement. He has also given me strategies to solve certain situations, so it is important that you have a notebook nearby for your annotations. The notebook you use here is only to be used during your Bible reading time and I suggest that you write the date each day indicating the chapter you have read and what God has shown you that day. At the end of the year you will see how He has taken you by the hand in every situation. It is a very nice and rewarding experience.

PRACTICE PRAISE AND WORSHIP CONTINUOUSLY

It is very important that you always have songs available to worship God. You can have them on your phone, on your computer, on your stereo, but the most important thing is that you have them in your heart. We do not need instruments, or special sound effects; all we need is to open our mouth and praise God. God does not care if you sing beautifully or horribly, or if you know the lyrics by heart or if you are inventing new songs from your heart. The only thing that matters to God is your heart—that you melt before His presence no matter what you are feeling. There are times when I worship the Lord with a smile on my face because everything is fine, but I also do it with tears of sadness when I have a problem or I am very tired or downcast by situations that come in my life.

One thing is always true: every time I praise Him, the mood I was in when I started becomes irrelevant. This is because by the time I finish, I am no longer crying out of sadness, but rather crying out of joy.

In a supernatural way, the Lord changes sadness into joy every time.

Not in vain does the Lord tell us:

"You have turned my mourning into joyful dancing. You have taken away my clothes of mourning and clothed me with joy" Psalm 30:11

We must take into account that when we praise the Lord, our emotional state changes because we no longer focus on how big our problem is, but on how big our God is. Suddenly, in a supernatural way, we begin to feel the strength and confidence that only He can give us. We no longer praise from our problematic situation, but from our position as sons and daughters loved by an all-powerful King. Very soon our spirit receives the certainty that, if our father loves us and is almighty, then everything will be fine. When we trust in Him, our faith increases and automatically changes our confession. Now we begin to speak by faith, and because faith pleases God, supernatural things begin to happen. Your life will change before your eyes when you constantly praise God. Look at what it says in Hebrews 13:15:

"Therefore, let us offer through Jesus a continual sacrifice of praise to God, proclaiming our allegiance to his name"

It is true that sometimes it is a sacrifice, many times you do not have any desire to praise; but I must warn you that many times that reluctance comes from the devil himself who does not want you to praise God because he knows how powerful praise is. Remember that Satan was in charge of praise in heaven until he rebelled against God and was expelled from heaven according to the book of Isaiah:

"How you are fallen from heaven, O shining star, son of the morning! You have been thrown down to the earth, you who destroyed the nations of the world. For you said to yourself, 'I will ascend to heaven and set my throne

above God's stars. I will preside on the mountain of the gods far away in the north. I will climb to the highest heavens and be like the Most High.' Instead, you will be brought down to the place of the dead, down to its lowest depths." Isaiah 14:12-15

Therefore, we have been warned. Be on guard and aware of the schemes of the enemy! When you feel discouraged and don't have any desire to praise the Lord, that is precisely when you have to press on and make yourself praise Him. Play a powerful worship song, open your mouth, get up off the chair and start dancing, walk, raise your hands to heaven and praise Him. Have an extravagant praise for the Lord. Do not let the devil steal the blessing that God has prepared for you. When you follow this recommendation, very soon you will be able to verify the faithfulness of God and your spirit will change and you will cry for joy in His presence. That extravagant and continuous adoration will take your life to levels unknown to you, and you will see with your own eyes that the will of God is good, pleasant and perfect as it says in Romans 12:2.

DECIDE TO MAKE GOD THE LORD OF ALL AREAS OF YOUR LIFE

This means that God commands everything concerning your life: your time, your finances, your work, your business, your family, your friendships, etc. And since the Lord is the one who commands, you obey because you understand that He knows better and wants the best for you.

The most common issue with believers is related to the lordship of Jesus in their whole life. They have no problem with Jesus being their Savior or their friend, but the problem comes when they try to accept Him as their Lord who commands all areas of their lives. As a result, we see believers who, even after years of attending a church, are still spiritual infants. They get upset and disobey God when He, for example, tells them: "stop speaking badly about your boss," "you must help your parents financially because they need you," "stop talking to that secretary because you will end up in adultery," etc. They do not want God as their Lord because they want to do what they want. We all start as infants, and that is to be expected, but we are also expected to grow. We read this clearly in 1 Peter 2:2:

"As newborn babes, desire the pure milk of the word, that you may grow thereby"

It is an invitation from God to desire His Word as a newborn child desires his mother's milk. Have you seen when a baby is hungry and wants to be fed? That baby cries desperately until it sticks to his mother's breast to eat. And one can see that the baby sucks hard until he/she is satisfied and falls asleep. A healthy baby is a hungry baby. A baby must eat to grow. Likewise, we must feed on the Word of God to grow.

We must read the Word, meditate on it, processing the truth it contains to learn to think and live by it.

God wants us to be doers of the Word, that is, to live according to what it is written:

"But be doers of the word, and not hearers only, deceiving yourselves." James 1:22

Remember that spiritual babies are hearers of the Word, but spiritual adults put all their effort into being doers of the Word. Spiritual adults seek to live according to the Word and accept the lordship of God in their lives. Spiritual adults know that growth is constant and therefore they study the Scriptures diligently because they know Jesus is their role model. Their goal is to grow "to the measure of the stature of the fullness of Christ" according to Ephesians:

"…until we all come to the unity of the faith and of the knowledge of the Son of God, to a perfect man, to the measure of the stature of the fullness of Christ" Ephesians 4:13

When our role model is Jesus we seek constant growth because we realize that the standard is very high.

God expects us to strive to grow steadily until we reach the stature of Christ.

DECIDE TO PURPOSELY WALK IN HOLINESS

The scripture in Hebrews 12:14 is very clear when it says that without holiness no one will see the Lord.

> *"Pursue peace with all people, and holiness, without which no one will see the Lord"* Hebrews 12:14

Holiness refers to being "separated" for Him. The Greek term that defines holiness is "hagiasmos" and means "separation," specifically the separation of the clean from the unclean.[1] In practicality, this refers to a person who separates themselves from bad things.

We, as His sons and daughters, are called to live in holiness—to be set apart for Him, to be different, to do things in a different way. The way to do this is simple and it is written in the Bible; hence, it is important that we renew our thoughts according to His Word. Look at what Leviticus says:

> *"And you shall be holy to Me, for I the LORD am holy, and have separated you from the peoples, that you should be Mine."* Leviticus 20:26

In that same chapter, God instructs His people against abortion, adultery, fornication, divination, witchcraft, and many other abominations. Not only does He give them instructions, but He also alerts them about the consequences and curses if they come to participate in those things. God wants us to be holy, that is to say, separated from all those practices that for many are normal but which He detests.

It is possible for someone to argue and say "well, that is old because it is written in the Old Testament, times have changed and it is different now." In case there is doubt, we see it again in the New Testament:

> *"because it is written, "Be holy, for I am holy."*
> 1 Peter 1:16

God wants us to set apart for Him. Decide to sanctify your hearing by only hearing things that edify you and bring you closer to God. For this reason, you must be very aware of the music you listen to and the conversations in which you participate. I remember the first time we bought our daughter a music listening device we made her promise that she would only listen to Christian music. From time to time my husband and I would verify that the agreement was being kept. This kept her from being influenced by all the unedifying ideology so common in pop culture, and also made her quite well versed in the edifying work of the musicians in the body of Christ. I would also recommend paying special attention to the well-known double meaning jokes that in the end are full of vulgarities and mundane ideas. Get away from those conversations because they will hurt you in the end.

At the same time, decide to sanctify your eyes and carefully select movies, TV shows, videos, books, and all other content through the lens of holiness. My husband and I took the television out of our home a long time ago, when our daughter was just starting high school. Back then, we noticed that although we had a fairly expensive and "complete" cable service, it was difficult to find a program with good values. Additionally, most ads had sensual content, disrespectful phrases, or financial mismanagement among other things. We also began to notice that our daughter was rushing to finish her homework and other chores just to spend hours sitting in front of the television set.

One day we decided to remove the cable and use the television for Christian movies and educational videos only. Our daughter was upset at first, but soon she began to read more, she learned to play the guitar, and was advanced to an accelerated program at school because her performance had surpassed her grade level. This sustained learning growth throughout the years ultimately landed her at an Ivy League school and in one of the best business programs in the world. She completed an undergraduate curriculum with a price tag of a quarter of a million dollars that was completely covered by the school.

Perhaps you may think that the decision to use the TV only for Christian films and educational videos was excessive or too radical, but I can assure you that it worked wonders for us and for our daughter. When we look back, we confirm it was an excellent decision. I highly recommend it especially if you have school-age children. Television just programs people to do things the world's way, and not God's way.

Do not get upset when they treat you as if you are exaggerating, outdated, fanatic, group breaker, or going against the flow or any other unpleasant names.

Please remember the scriptures:

> *"Of course, your former friends are surprised when you no longer plunge into the flood of wild and destructive things they do. So they slander you."* 1 Peter 4:4

> *"So don't be surprised, dear brothers and sisters, if the world hates you."* 1 John 3:13

So do not be surprised when they make fun of you or no longer invite you to their activities. Those friendships do not suit you. Just be brave and do things God's way. The Lord will give you wonderful friendships that I call "divine connections," because they are people that He brings near you for the fulfillment of His purposes in your life.

WATCH YOUR THOUGHTS DILIGENTLY

In all circumstances, it is very important that your thoughts are subject to the obedience of Christ. You must take into account the source of your thoughts because there are three different sources: God, yourself, or your enemy the devil. The thoughts of God will always be aligned with His Word because He never contradicts His Word. Your thoughts are not always yours; in fact, they may come from the enemy (who always speaks in first person) making you think that it is you. When we are not sure about the origin of a thought, then we must ask the Holy Spirit.

In difficult situations, when unpleasant thoughts come to my mind and I know those thoughts are not from God, I quickly open my mouth and quote scriptures out loud "I take every thought captive to the obedience of Christ." It is written:

> "Casting down arguments and every high thing that exalts itself against the knowledge of God, bringing every thought into captivity to the obedience of Christ"
> 2 Corinthians 10:5

You will have negative or unpleasant thoughts from time to time, but you should not entertain them.

Martin Luther said: "You cannot keep birds from flying over your head, but you can keep them from building a nest in your hair"

I once heard that adultery begins in the mind and it is consummated in the bed. So many infidelities and disorders begin by entertaining an inappropriate thought.

> "Finally, brethren, whatever things are true, whatever things are noble, whatever things are just, whatever things are pure, whatever things are lovely, whatever things are of good report, if there is any virtue and if there is anything praiseworthy—meditate on these things."
> Philippians 4:8

The Lord wants the best for us, and that is why he gives us clear and precise instructions about how our thoughts should be.

NOTES

1 Robert Vargas, Tell me what you hear & I'll Tell You Who You Are (my own translation since book has not yet been translated into English), p. 36.

Chapter 5

Are you prudent with your words?

Surely you have heard a popular saying, something like this: "tell me who you are with and I will tell you who you are." I have another personal saying and it says: "let me hear the way you talk and I'll tell you how you think."

When I hear someone complaining or saying words that do not bless their life, I say to myself: "if they only knew that it is just a matter of time before they see what they are declaring coming to pass." You have noticed those people who say "I get sick every time people in the office get sick," or "I catch every little virus that goes around;" Aren't they always sick? And what about those who say "I never have enough money," or "by the time I get paid, I have already spent all my money;" aren't they always short of money? Let me tell you, it is not a coincidence. In this chapter we will discover that our spoken words are very powerful.

It is only when we know that our words have power that we really strive to control what we say, because we know that there are consequences.

Those consequences can be in our favor or against us. That is to say, these consequences can be a blessing, but they can also be a curse for our lives.

We saw in the previous chapter that our thoughts guide our actions, and our actions determine our present and our future. So, there is a direct connection between our thoughts and our reality. You may be asking yourself, how does this happen? The answer is simple: what is in your mind, sooner or later, will come out through your mouth; and what comes out of your mouth, sooner or later, will materialize in your life.

It is important to clarify that I am not talking about New Age belief systems that encourage positive thinking and positive confession. I am not talking about the so-called "law of attraction" either. All of these, including the Silva method, hypnosis and others, are evil practices disguised as "relaxation methods" and we should not lend our ears to them or partake of them in any form. Though these New Age activities may seem innocent, they are fundamentally satanic and therefore very dangerous. Part of the reason for this is because many exercises call for the person to "empty their mind," making them susceptible and open to receiving demonic influences. Our mind cannot be blank; instead, it must be alert at all times and be continuously filled with the Word of God.

The power of our words is validated in the Bible.

"Death and life are in the power of the tongue, and those who love it will eat its fruit." **Proverbs 18:21**

"If you want to enjoy life and see many happy days, keep your tongue from speaking evil and your lips from telling lies." **1 Peter 3:10**

Scripture tells us clearly that our spoken words have the power to kill and to give life, that is, to destroy something or to produce something. Therefore, if we want to see good things happen, then we must restrain and control our tongue.

Scripture also tells us about the power of agreement:

"I also tell you this: If two of you agree here on earth concerning anything you ask, my Father in heaven will do it for you." **Matthew 18:19**

The power of agreement is a biblical principle that, when used wisely, will give us wonderful results. We can think of a "biblical principle" as a God-ordained law that specifies how things function. In the spiritual realm, they are analogous to the laws of nature. Take the law of gravity, for example. Imagine that I am standing with an object in my hand; if I let it go, irreversibly that object will fall to the ground. This will happen even if I pray and fast for three days for this not to happen. God designed the law of gravity and no matter what I do this law will always be fulfilled. Similarly, the law of agreement works all the time because God has designed it as such.

> *The law of agreement says that when two or more agree on something, it will be done.*

In *Matthew 18:19* Jesus tells us to be in agreement with God. To agree with God means to agree with His Word. But it is also important to note that we can be in agreement with the forces of evil and that will be done as well.

Summarizing, we have learned that our tongue has the power to create and to destroy; we also have stated that the power of agreement works for both good and evil. So, when a person says "I get sick when people I work with get sick," that person is using the power of his tongue to create the sickness in his body. Moreover, he is activating the power of agreement, linking his confession with the forces of evil since that confession is contrary to the word of God. Scripture, according to *1 Peter 2:24*, says that *"we are healed by the wounds of Christ"* and that *"He personally carried our sins in his body on the cross so that we can be dead to sin and live for what is right. By his wounds you are healed."*

Let us study another example. When a person says "I never have enough money," that person is using the power of the tongue to create financial lack and also activating the power of agreement. That person is linking with the forces of evil because his confession is contrary to the word of God, which says that He will supply all of our needs. Please remember *Philippians 4:19 "And my God shall supply all your need according to His riches in glory by Christ Jesus."*

I must confess that learning these principles was not easy for me; I was accustomed to talking without thinking too much about what I said. It took a lot of effort, systematic study of the Word of God and strict discipline on my part to change this. As I was learning, whenever I heard words coming out of my lips that I knew were not going to result in blessings, I immediately corrected myself by making a confession according to God's Word. Let me give you an example. This happened a long time ago, when I was still single and longed to marry a powerful man of God who would love Him more than me. When friends at church or at work would ask me if I was married I would say "no" because in reality I was not. But the Lord began to reveal to me things concerning the power of my tongue and the principle of agreement.

Then when the "no" would come out of my mouth, I started immediately correcting myself and saying, "yes by faith." This answer confused people because they insisted by asking again: "but are you married or not?" to which I responded again: "yes by faith." I had understood that when I said "yes" I would be using the power of my tongue to give life and create my marriage and when I said "by faith," I would be bound in agreement with God because His Word says that I should call the things that are not as though they were, according to *Romans 4:17 "as it is written: …God, who gives life to the dead and calls those things which do not exist as though they did."*

You probably ask, but Silvia, does that mean that I should lie? And the answer is an emphatic no! The Lord detests lies. This has nothing to do with lying; rather, it is about speaking by faith attached to the Word of God. God commands us to speak by faith and the Word tells us to call things that are not as if they were.

Robert Vargas, a Venezuelan Pastor and Teacher, had an impressive revelation on this topic because he states that God told him "your words are legal documents, written in the spiritual realm," and even confirmed it with *Psalm 45:1 "....my tongue is like the pen of a skillful poet."*[1]

Be mindful that it is our tongue that writes our future.

It depends on us. Will we align ourselves with the Word of God for our life, or will we lose the blessings and purpose He has for us?

Additionally, we must remember that His word will be fulfilled:

"It is the same with my word. I send it out, and it always produces fruit. It will accomplish all I want it to, and it will prosper everywhere I send it." Isaiah 55:11

In his book *Refrain Your Tongue From Speaking Evil*, Pastor Robert explains according to Psalm 1

"Blessed is the man
Who walks not in the counsel of the ungodly,
Nor stands in the path of sinners,
Nor sits in the seat of the scornful;
But his delight is in the law of the LORD,
And in His law he meditates day and night."

This begins with a blessing for those who meet these requirements:

1. Do not walk on bad advice
2. Do not walk in the way of sinners
3. Do not sit with mockers

The wicked, the sinner and the scoffer all speak words that do not edify spiritually. Normally, what we continually listen to is what we are going to talk about; therefore, the man (meaning all human kind) who does not associate himself with people of this sort (talking trash and speaking evil like them) is blessed.

The second verse of this same Psalm says *"But his delight is in the law of the LORD, and in His law he meditates day and night."* Someone could say that he does not see anything related to the confession of the word in this verse, however, observing the Hebrew (the original language of the old testament) we will notice something else.

The word "meditates" in the original is "hagah," which means "to repeat quietly with a soft sound."

We could then read this verse as: "But in the word of God is his delight and he *repeats it quietly* day and night."

> *We will be blessed when we do not have the three types of friendships verse one speaks about, and when day and night we are confessing His Word.*

But the good results do not end there. Look at what it says next:

> *"He shall be like a tree*
> *Planted by the rivers of water,*
> *That brings forth its fruit in its season,*
> *Whose leaf also shall not wither;*
> *And whatever he does shall prosper."* Psalm 1:3

Blessed be the word of God for the great results it can give. As a tree planted by streams of water, so will it be for he who, day and night, confesses the word of our King. Decide now to spend more time in the Word, scrutinize it deeply and then put it in your mouth. Stop talking about the words the devil wants you to talk about once and for all.

God needs here on earth a church full of power; that will only be possible if His church has a biblical and supernatural language.[2]

With great joy I share today that God granted my wishes and for many years I have been married to that powerful man for whom I prayed without ceasing and with unwavering faith.

> *I encourage you! Put the word of God in your mouth and you will see your life prospered.*

Use your tongue to bless your life, your family, your spouse, your finances and all that God has given you in stewardship.

NOTES

1 Robert Vargas, Refrain your tongue from speaking Evil (my own translation since book has not yet been translated into English), p. 3.

2 Ibid p. 34-36

Chapter 6

Do you honor God
with your finances?

Maybe you're wondering and asking yourself "what do my finances have to do with my keeping my deliverance and walking in victory?" Well, that is precisely what we will discover in this chapter. Your finances, which really are not yours because everything belongs to God, play a decisive role.

I mentioned in chapter four that "spiritual babies" have trouble accepting the lordship of Jesus Christ, for the simple reason that they want to do what they see fit. Spiritual babies do not want to surrender their finances to the lordship of Jesus Christ and therefore they are opening a giant door for the enemy to steal what God wants to give them.

In this chapter it will be clear to us that:

- Everything belongs to God
- What He gives to us is to be administered
- If we rob God we get ourselves into serious problems
- God wants us to be prosperous

EVERYTHING BELONGS TO GOD

Let us look at some verses to reinforce this truth.

"The earth is the Lord's, and all its fullness, the world and those who dwell therein." Psalm 24:1

"For every beast of the forest is Mine, and the cattle on a thousand hills. I know all the birds of the mountains, and the wild beasts of the field are Mine. If I were hungry, I would not tell you; for the world is Mine, and all its fullness." Psalm 50:10-12

"The silver is Mine, and the gold is Mine,' says the Lord of hosts." Haggai 2:8

What He gives to us is to be stewarded. He gave us the responsibility to administer all we have.

"Then the Lord God took the man and put him in the garden of Eden to tend and keep it." Genesis 2:15

And the Lord said, *"Who then is that faithful and wise steward, whom his master will make ruler over his household, to give them their portion of food in due season? Blessed is that servant whom his master will find so doing when he comes."* Luke 12:42-43

In this last verse we also see that there will come a time when He will ask us to account for what we did with everything He gave us to administer.

IF WE ROB GOD, WE GET OURSELVES INTO SERIOUS PROBLEMS

We saw in the first chapter of this guide that according to Ephesians 4:27 the devil can be given place to cause problems in our lives. Definitely mismanaged finances can give place, i.e., legal right, to the devil to disturb our income or any other area in our lives. A "legal right" is "what feeds" the devil and gives him permission to stay.[1]

Something basic that a Christian must do with his finances is to tithe. If it is true that everything is from God, we must give our church ten percent of our gross income (before taxes, health insurance and other deductions). That ten percent belongs to God and we must give it to Him if we want Him to defend us against the enemy. If we do not tithe nor give our offerings, we are robbing God.

Let me tell you that there has always been a great problem among the people of God because many have not wanted to accept that all God gives to them is to be administered according to His will. And His will is that we tithe and give our offerings, with the guidance of the Holy Spirit.

It may surprise you to know that only a small percentage of God's people tithe, and it is no wonder that so many have financial problems. For some reason they have decided that tithing is no longer necessary because they say it is an Old Testament practice that has been rendered obsolete. Very soon we will see that this is not true, tithing is also a practice of the New Testament and it is in force today as well. Remember that God is the same yesterday, today and forever!

We will go straight to the Word and will take a look at Malachi 3:8-12

DO NOT ROB GOD

> *"Will man rob God? Yet you are robbing me. But you say, 'How have we robbed you?' In your tithes and contributions. You are cursed with a curse, for you are robbing me, the whole nation of you. Bring the full tithe into the storehouse, that there may be food in my house. And thereby put me to the test, says the* LORD *of hosts, if I will not open the windows of heaven for you and pour down for you a blessing until there is no more need. I will rebuke the devourer for you, so that it will not destroy the fruits of your soil, and your vine in the field shall not fail to bear, says the* LORD *of hosts. Then all nations will call you blessed, for you will be a land of delight, says the* LORD *of hosts."*

It is important to note that in verse 9 the Lord tells us that we will be cursed if we do not tithe. Nothing good comes from a curse and examples of the consequences of disobedience abound in Deuteronomy 28. In verse 10 the Lord challenges us by encouraging us to test him. In other words, He is asking us to tithe so He can prove His power to us. Then in verse 11 he tells us that He himself will keep the enemy away, and that He will prohibit the enemy to destroy what it is ours.

Now, let's take a look at the New Testament:

> *"I fast twice a week; I give tithes of all that I possess"*
> Luke 18:12

Here Jesus shares with his disciples about two people: a Pharisee and a tax collector. I invite you to read it in your Bible. In this narrative it is very clear that tithing is also a common practice in New Testament times. Notice the expression "I give tithes of all that I possess." In addition, it is very evident that tithing works.

Tithing is a biblical principle; it is a spiritual equivalent of a natural law, like that of the law of gravity as mentioned in the previous chapter. God establishes principles in his Word knowing that if we fulfill them, it will be good for us.

If you want to avoid the curses mentioned in Malachi, and you want God to rebuke the devourer, then you must tithe.

Please allow me to share a personal testimony that appears in another one of my books[2] regarding my early days as an immigrant in the United States. This happened many years ago, but it serves as a powerful testimony of God's faithfulness when we do things His way.

This was in the months shortly after our arrival in the United States, when my daughter was very young and my income very small. One morning before going to church I made my grocery list and, after estimating the cost of that week's run, I realized I had a choice to make: either I gave my contribution (tithe) to the church or I bought groceries for the week; there was not enough money to do both. Then, I asked myself, what does God say about this?

> "'Bring all the tithes into the storehouse so there will be enough food in my Temple. If you do,' says the Lord of Heaven's Armies, 'I will open the windows of heaven for you. I will pour out a blessing so great you won't have enough room to take it in! Try it! Put me to the test! Your crops will be abundant, for I will guard them from insects and disease. Your grapes will not fall from the vine before they are ripe,' says the Lord of Heaven's Armies. 'Then all nations will call you blessed, for your land will be such a delight,' says the Lord of Heaven's Armies." Malachi 3:10-12

Well, it was very clear; He says that I must take my contribution to the temple. I must confess that I had a conversation with God; I said, "Lord, this is not easy" and I felt that He told me "I did not say it was going to be easy."

Once again, I thought about Abraham, the thought of having to sacrifice his only son must have been tremendously difficult. I also remembered that his obedience brought blessings upon his life and that of many others. With God's Word, and with Abraham's example in mind, I also decided to obey. We managed to go to church and once there, with a knot in my stomach, but with a happy and confident heart, I put my tithe on the offering tray trusting that something good would come.

After church, some friends invited us to eat and then we went back to the little room we were renting at the time. At about three o'clock in the afternoon somebody knocked on the door. I was not expecting any visitors, so I was astonished to see someone from the church standing outside holding several bags. I asked: "And what is this?" And this person says to me: "I was buying food for my family and I felt in my heart I should buy groceries for you as well."

I thanked them and after they left, my little princess and I started crying with happiness. That person had brought us food not for a week, as I used to buy, but for three weeks! How awesome! I had tested God, as he says in His Word to do, and He had fulfilled His Word by giving me much more than I could have bought myself.

Step by step, hand in hand with God, we have advanced more and more since then. We continue to believe in what the Bible says, and strive to put it into practice – acting by faith, knowing that it is not easy but that it is possible. Today, with economic stability and even a house of our own by the grace of God, we continue walking by faith in every area He calls us to.

I encourage you to tithe and to accept God's challenge for you.

You will be surprised and you'll see your economy go from good to better, just as I did.

GOD WANTS US TO BE PROSPEROUS

The prosperity that God gives us is for the purpose of living the abundant life that He promises in His word and for the expansion of His Kingdom here on earth.

> *"The thief does not come except to steal, and to kill, and to destroy. I have come that they may have life, and that they may have it more abundantly."* John 10:10

Here we see that Christ came so that we would have life in abundance and that includes economic prosperity.

> *"Let the Lord be magnified, Who has pleasure in the prosperity of His servant."* Psalm 35:27

God delights in our wellbeing. He is pleased when we are doing well, including financially.

Once I heard somebody ask these questions: what good is there when we cannot pay for electricity, or water, or phone bills? And what welfare is there when we cannot pay for the education of our children? What benefit is there when we cannot pay the mortgage or monthly rent on our house or when we cannot buy groceries?

When we cannot pay for things, then there is no happiness. God does not like it when we cannot pay for what we need; He is a good Father who is pleased to see us prosper.

And my God shall supply all your need according to His riches in glory by Christ Jesus. Philippians 4:19

Here we see that it is God who supplies according to His riches; and we have already seen that His riches abound greatly in that all is His. We have a super, hyper, mega millionaire Father!

"And you shall remember the Lord your God, for it is He who gives you power to get wealth, that He may establish His covenant which He swore to your fathers, as it is this day". Deuteronomy 8:18

He is the one who gives us the power to make riches. It does not say that riches will come down from heaven without you doing anything. You have an important role to play in all this, which includes praying, studying, working, etc. He will help you as you work. He will give you good ideas, new clients, edifying working relationships, etc., He will do it because He says it in His word.

"And God is able to make all grace abound toward you, that you, always having all sufficiency in all things, may have an abundance for every good work." 2 Corinthians 9:8

God wants us to be prosperous, not only for ourselves but also that we may be a blessing to others as well. God knows your heart and if you want only your own wellbeing, it is likely that you will not enjoy the riches that He has for you.

Remember that God's wealth is perfect and does not bring sadness.

Robert Henderson, in his book *Caused Blessings* explains that we can intentionally seek to be blessed by following the strategies outlined in the Word regarding prosperity. Henderson explains that just as God made the law of gravity, which affects everything around us, He also made laws for the multiplication of money. Two of these laws are the law of Sowing and Reaping, and the law of Giving; both work hand and hand.

He explains that a farmer who sows on a ten-acre piece of land will never expect to harvest twenty acres worth of produce. What he may look to do instead is to sell the crops he harvested from the ten acres of land, and purchase a land of twenty acres. Then he sows this land of twenty acres, and with that harvest he can then buy a thirty-acre plot of land. In this way, he continues to enlarge his territory, which at the same time increases his harvest. This can happen because the seed that is sown always bears fruit; this can be thirty, sixty and one hundred percent. Let's look:

"But others fell on good ground and yielded a crop: some a hundredfold, some sixty, some thirty". Matthew 13:8

The Word is clear when it says that the seed will bear fruit at thirty, sixty and one hundred percent. That is to say that when I sow, I will always reap.

This is only logical; if no one has sown apples in the backyard of your house, there would be no reason to expect to see an apple tree or to eat of its fruits. The principle here is very clear: sowing is required. If you want to harvest apples, you must sow apples. If you want to harvest money, you must sow money; not in the backyard of your house but in ministries where God is present (on good ground, in fertile land).

It is very important to note that tithing is not sowing. Your tithe is not a seed; your tithe is God's money and goes to the church or to the ministry that feeds you spiritually, as we read earlier. For example:

If you earn $1,000, and you tithe $100, you must understand that you have sown $0.

If you only tithe, your finances will not improve, i.e., you will always be at the level of "bare necessities;" that is, to go from paycheck to paycheck, just enough to cover bills.

THE SEED IS THE OFFERING

What counts as the seed is the offering you bring.

The size of the offering is directly proportional to the size of the seed.

Although initially your seed may be small, as you harvest, you will have more seed to sow. Just like in the example that we just saw about the farmer; in time your sowing will be bigger and therefore your harvest will also increase. This is supported by the Word with the following two verses:

"Give, and it will be given to you: good measure, pressed down, shaken together, and running over will be put into your bosom. For with the same measure that you use, it will be measured back to you." Luke 6:38

"And God is able to make all grace abound toward you, that you, always having all sufficiency in all things, may have an abundance for every good work". 2 Corinthians 9:8

If we look closely, in Luke 6:38 we will see that there are four types of measures:

1. Good measure
2. Pressed down
3. Shaken together
4. Running over

2 Corinthians 9:8 speaks of

- Everything you need = **Good measure** = first level where you have enough
- A lot to share = **Running over** = level of prosperity where you have to spare

Robert Henderson explains that as our sowing increases, so does our harvest. We begin with only the necessary, i.e., "good measure." Then, as we continue to move up, we can intentionally be blessed and move to the "pressed down" measure, then to "shaken together" measure, and then finally to "running over" measure as long as our sowing increases.

> "We determine how much comes back to us, just like a farmer determines how much harvest he gets by how much seed he sows."[3]

I can say that I am truly living God's strategy for prosperity, and I again invite you to believe Him. He knows more than we do, and He wants us to be prosperous so that we can show His love by helping others and extending His Kingdom on this earth.

It is very important to take into account that what we want is the blessing of God. There are many people with riches, but also with plenty of drama and sadness in their lives. We do not want that.

> We want the prosperity that comes from God and brings no sadness.

"The blessing of the Lord makes one rich,
And He adds no sorrow with it." **Proverbs 10:22**

NOTES

1. Doris M. Wagner, how to cast out demons, p. 60.
2. Silvia Sauve, Immigration, who has the last word (my own translation), p. 115-117.
3. Robert Henderson, Caused Blessing, p. 114.

Chapter 7

Spiritual Discipline

Very often we see that the Word of God commands us to be diligent and courageous; therefore, we need to be very disciplined. Let's look at what the Apostle Paul says:

> *"Do you not know that those who run in a race all run, but one receives the prize? Run in such a way that you may obtain it. And everyone who competes for the prize is temperate in all things. Now they do it to obtain a perishable crown, but we for an imperishable crown. Therefore I run thus: not with uncertainty. Thus I fight: not as one who beats the air. But I discipline my body and bring it into subjection, lest, when I have preached to others, I myself should become disqualified."* 1 Corinthians 9:24-27

Discipline is a serious thing. When I read this passage, I think of the athletes who train for the Olympics—how they undergo countless hours of intense training, how they forgo many types of food, curb sleep, and sacrifice time with friends and family in order to devote the necessary time for practicing. In short, they sacrifice a long list of pleasures in order that they may achieve the goal.

We also see what Jesus said to the disciples:

"Then Jesus said to His disciples, 'If anyone desires to come after Me, let him deny himself, and take up his cross, and follow Me.'" Matthew 16:24

Let us be determined to carry out the spiritual discipline necessary to continue walking in freedom and victory.

First of all, I invite you to thank the Lord for setting you free:

- Thank you, Jesus, for making me free – Jesus came to deliver the captives according to Luke 4:18

- Thank you, Lord, because I am a new creation

  "Therefore, if anyone is in Christ, he is a new creation; old things have passed away; behold, all things have become new." 2 Corinthians 5:17

- Thank you, Lord, for giving me the desire and the will to keep my freedom from all oppression and for living the abundant life that you have for me.

  "... I (Jesus) have come that they may have life, and that they may have it more abundantly." John 10:10

Next, I invite you to commit yourself to the Lord in this new spiritual discipline.

Dear God, I promise to:

- Pray, be in your Presence, immerse myself in the river of your Spirit and feed my mind and my soul with your Word by reading at least one chapter of the Bible every day.

- Fast, according to the guidance of the Holy Spirit.

- Diligently pay attention to what I see (television, movies, internet, etc.), what I hear (radio, music, conversations), and what I do (work, fun and all activities) in order that all of these would bring honor and glory to your name. That these would all put a smile on your face, knowing that you are with me at all times and in all places.

- Carefully choose my friends. I may intentionally share with all people, but my friends will be people who love You, who fear You, who serve You and who put You first in their lives for everything.

- Live passionately for You—calling bad what You call bad, and calling good what You call good.

- Ask for Your wisdom knowing that you will give it to me according to James 1:5 so that I may know and understand Your times and Your will.

- To fulfill the Great Commission according to Matthew 28:19-20 by winning souls for Christ and teaching them all that You have taught me.

CONFESSIONS FOR OVERCOMERS

I invite you to declare:

My body is a temple for the Holy Spirit (1 Cor. 6:19), redeemed (Eph. 1:7; Ps. 107:2), cleansed (1 John 1:7), and sanctified by the Blood of Jesus (Heb. 13:12). My members, the parts of my body, are instruments of righteousness (Rom. 6:13), yielded to God for His service and for His glory. The devil has no place in me, no power over me, no unsettled claims against me. All has been settled by the Blood of Jesus (Rom. 8:33-34). I overcome Satan by the Blood of the Lamb and by the word of my testimony, and I love not my life unto the death (Rev. 12:11). My body is for the Lord and the Lord is for my body (1 Cor.6:13).

I am not just an ordinary man/woman; I am a son/daughter of the living God. I am an heir of God and a joint heir with Jesus Christ. I am part of a chosen generation, a royal priesthood, a holy nation; I am one of God's people (Gal. 4:6-7; 1 Peter 2:9).

I am not under guilt or condemnation. There is no condemnation for those in Christ Jesus. Satan is a liar. I will not listen to his accusations. No weapon formed against me will prosper (Rom. 8:1; Is. 54:17).

My mind is being renewed by the Word of God. I pull down strongholds, I cast down imaginations, and I bring every thought captive to the obedience of Christ (2 Cor. 10:4; Rom. 12:2).

I am accepted in the Beloved. If God is for me, who can be against me? Nothing can separate me from the love of Christ (Rom. 8:35-39).

Satan is defeated: The Son of God came into the world to destroy the works of the devil. No longer will he oppress me. I defeat Satan and all demons by the Blood of the Lamb, by the Word of my testimony, not loving my life even unto death. I submit to God; I resist the devil and he must flee from me **NOW!!** (Rev. 12:11, James 4:7-8).

No temptation will overtake me that is not common to man. But God is faithful; He will not let me be tempted beyond my strength but with the temptation will also provide a way of escape that I may be able to endure it (1 Cor. 10:13).

I give no place to fear in my life. That which a man fears comes upon him. The fear of man brings a snare, but perfect love casts out fear. I sought the Lord and He heard me and delivered me from all my fears (2 Tim. 1:7; 1 John 4:18; Ps. 34:4).

The Lord is my light and my salvation; whom shall I fear? The Lord is the strength of my life; of whom shall I be afraid? God is my refuge and strength, a very present help in trouble. Therefore, I will not fear (Ps. 27:1; Ps. 46:1-2).

I am not ashamed of the gospel, for it is the power of God unto salvation to those who believe (Rom.1:16).

I am a believer, not a doubter. I have faith towards God. My faith is not in myself or in the realm of my feelings, but in a living God who will never fail me nor forsake me. I walk by faith and not by sight (Heb. 11:1, 6).

I will be anxious for nothing. He will keep me in perfect peace, for my mind is stayed upon Him (Phil 4:6-7, Isa. 26:3).

I choose this day to live by faith, to walk by faith, and to see with the eyes of faith. I will go from faith to faith, from strength to strength, from glory to glory (Rom. 1:17, 2 Cor. 5:7).

I look not to the healing but to the healer: Jesus Christ, My Lord. My body is for the Lord and the Lord is for my body. He took away my sickness and carried all my diseases. By His stripes I am healed. The same spirit that raised Christ from the dead is at work in my body, giving me life (1 Peter 2:24, Matt. 8:16-17).

The credit of these confessions is given to Dr. William Sudduth, taken from Deliverance Training Manual p.70-71. This reflection is a modified version of his work.

Epilogue

Confrontation of demons is actually a small part of the deliverance process. Deliverance is more about developing a close relationship with the Lord and building up the new life in Christ than confronting demons. With this in mind, walking closely with the Lord after the sessions have concluded, becomes the priority.[1]

STAYING FREE (WALKING IT OUT)

Deliverance is not the end, it is the beginning. We receive deliverance from past hurts, wounds and bondages, and then we press on toward the goal. As we do so, we need to understand that no matter what our nationality, or where we are from, we have a new citizenship. We are no longer of this world; our citizenship is in heaven and we are just pilgrims passing through this world. Knowing this will help us to keep our focus on the goal. We should also note that the enemy is not going to give up. There will still be temptations, trials, tests, and attacks. When we are under an attack, we need to know: "This too will pass." Everything in this life is temporal.

In walking out deliverance, a couple of scriptures comes to mind – first is Matthew 12:43-45, "When an evil spirit comes out of a man, it goes through arid places seeking rest and does not find it. Then it says, 'I will return to the house I left.' When it arrives, it finds the house unoccupied, swept clean, and put in order. Then it goes and takes with it seven other spirits more wicked than itself, and they go in and live there. And the final condition of that man is worse than the first. That is how it will be with this wicked generation." We want to make sure if and when that spirit returns, he finds that house full of the Holy Spirit and the power of God. To do this we must be baptized in the Holy Spirit and we must be full of the Word of God.

The next scripture is John 5:1-15, the story of the man at the pool of Bethesda. In verse 8, Jesus said to him, "Get up! Pick up your mat and walk" and the man was instantly cured. Following in verse 14 it says, "Later Jesus found him at the temple and said to him, 'See, you are well again. Stop sinning or something worse may happen to you'" (NIV). Most bondages come in through sin; and most spirits and strongholds are fed by sin. So, to walk out our deliverance and to stay free we too should go and sin no more!

We should be people of forgiveness, letting no root of bitterness spring up in us. Hebrews 12:14 says, "pursue peace with all people." Also, we should change old habits. I believe sin, as well as bad habits, open the door for the devil to put hooks in us. So, we need to ask God to show us any and all bad habits so we can break them. To walk in freedom, we have to choose to walk in the truth of the word of God and not by feelings. Feelings are up and down and if we walk by our feelings, we too will be up and down. We need to walk by faith, and in the Spirit—then we will walk in freedom. Revelation 12:11 says, "we are overcomers by the Blood of the Lamb and the word of our testimony." Our testimony reminds us of where we came from and what God has delivered us from. After ministering deliverance make sure they have cleaned out their home from all junk from the past. Encourage them to get rid of any and all ungodly tapes, CD's or videos, books, pictures, magazines, letters, photos, knickknacks, idols, witchcraft items, Masonic items and jewelry, and of course any articles of affection from an affair or any ungodly relationship. If they will ask the Holy Spirit, He will lead them and guide them, and if they are in doubt—get rid of it. The person who has been set free should have already done this.

If they have not been water baptized they need to be. Statistically, most new Christians who back slide were never baptized. Baptism is a command, not an option. The next thing is getting tied into a good church and becoming accountable to someone; a cell group leader, a pastor, or a mature brother or sister in the Lord. They should get plugged in and start serving in the church. Lastly, do not wait for the enemy to attack; the best defense is a good offense. Get into the word, pray every day and put on the full armor of God according to Ephesians chapter 6, and advance the kingdom of God. Witness, testify, walk and talk Jesus and above all else, **guard your thoughts**. You **are** what you think. Know that the battlefield is your mind; take authority over it, walk in freedom, and **stay free**![2]

NOTES

1. Deliverance on Purpose – Power Principles that Unlock Your Destiny, Dr. Ernie Sauve Jr., 2018, p. 160.
2. Deliverance Training Manual, Dr. William Sudduth, p. 69. This is a modified version of his work.

Appendix 1

Jesus your Savior

"How God anointed Jesus of Nazareth with the Holy Spirit and with power, who went about doing good and healing all who were oppressed by the devil, for God was with Him" Acts 10:38

The only way to walk in freedom is by having Jesus live in your heart. When you have invited him to be part of your life, He dwells in you and is the one who dictates the guidelines of your thoughts and actions. In your heart there must be a desire for change, a desire to be different, a conviction that you cannot do things on your own and that the only power to change your circumstances is found in God.

God has a **purpose** for your life. He wants you to live in peace here and with Him for all eternity according to John 3:16:

"For God so loved the world that He gave His only begotten Son, that whoever believes in Him should not perish but have everlasting life"

There is a **difficulty** and that is that our sins separate us from the glory of God and condemn us to an eternity without Him:

> *"For all have sinned and fall short of the glory of God"*
> Romans 3:23

There is nothing that by our efforts we can do. Our good works cannot erase our sins nor can they buy our salvation.

> *"For by grace you have been saved through faith, and that not of yourselves; it is the gift of God, not of works, lest anyone should boast"* Ephesians 2:8-9

There is a **solution** and it is Christ; Jesus is the only way. His redeeming work accomplished on the cross bought your salvation. He died and was resurrected on the third day for you! He paid the price in your place.

> *"In Him we have redemption through His blood, the forgiveness of sins, according to the riches of His grace"* Ephesians 1:7

> *"Jesus said to him, 'I am the way, the truth, and the life. No one comes to the Father except through Me.'"* John 14:6

Now the **choice** is yours. If you choose Jesus, your sins will be erased and you will spend eternity with Him in heaven. First, believe that Christ paid for your sins on the cross. Next, repent and ask God for forgiveness for what you know you have done wrong. And finally, with heartfelt words, open your mouth and invite him to dwell in your heart as your Lord and Savior.

> *"Most assuredly, I say to you, he who hears My word and believes in Him who sent Me has everlasting life, and shall not come into judgment, but has passed from death into life."* John 5:24

> *"...if you confess with your mouth the Lord Jesus and believe in your heart that God has raised Him from the dead, you will be saved. For with the heart one believes unto righteousness, and with the mouth confession is made unto salvation."* Romans 10:9-10

If you have made the decision to invite Jesus Christ into your live, then you can pray this little prayer below, or something similar.

> **"Lord my God, I know that I am a sinner and I need You to forgive me of my sins. I believe in my heart that Jesus Christ is your Son and that He died on the cross for my sins and that He rose on the third day and is with You now. I repent of all my sins; I invite you my Christ to come into my heart; I receive you as my Lord and Savior."**

Congratulations! You have made the most important decision of your life!

This is the beginning of a new life, a new birth. From now on, I invite you to feed your spirit with the Word of

God, reading the Bible daily. Additionally, I encourage you to talk to God in prayer and make special effort in making new friends who love God and want to please Him.

I pray that God will guide you in this new journey and that you will allow yourself to be guided by Him, towards the wonderful purpose He has for your life. From my own experience, I can testify that it is the best thing that can happen to you.

Appendix 2

About the author

Silvia graduated as an Electronic Engineer in Denver, Colorado, USA. and she also studied advanced Finances in Venezuela. Her conversion impacted many people as she immediately got immersed in Studies of the Old and New Testaments, Intense Discipleship, Deliverance and Victorious Life in Christ. She served in her local church in Venezuela and with her radio program *The Voice of Hope*, many souls came to the feet of Christ. In 2017, she completed her Master's Degree in Practical Ministry with Wagner University, California. Silvia is known as a Deliverance minister, prayer warrior and effective counselor.

In 2008, Silvia and her husband Dr. Ernest Sauve Jr., founded Daystream Ministries International, whose mission is to share the fresh and anointed Word of God with the purpose of provoking rains of revival and healing. They complement each other very well and bring experience, wisdom and knowledge to the ministry. They specialize in the ministry of deliverance under the leadership of Dr. Bill Sudduth, a giant in the area of deliverance and revival. Ernest and Silvia are the Hispanic Ambassadors of ISDM – International Society of Deliverance Ministries – isdmministers.org

Silvia and Ernest live in Florida USA and are working intensely worldwide, equipping the saints with training seminars and activating deliverance teams. – daystream.org

Appendix 3

How to Contact me

If you have any comments, questions or invitations you can write to silvia@daystream.org

You can also visit our page: daystream.org

Available conferences:

- Deliverance on Purpose Level I (How to be free from the oppressions of the devil)
- Deliverance on Purpose Level II (Training on Deliverance and Healing)
- Deliverance on Purpose Level III (Hands on training activating deliverance teams)

Appendix 4

The International Society of

Deliverance Ministers

The International Society of Deliverance Ministers (ISDM) was established in 2003 as an outgrowth of the Apostolic Roundtable of Deliverance Ministers (ARDM), founded in 2000. ARDM was originally convened under the leadership of C. Peter and Doris Wagner with the view of helping recognized deliverance ministers connect with each other, build personal relationships, learn from and encourage one another, and create a structure for accountability.

After a number of annual meetings, it became evident that ARDM was serving a valuable purpose, but that a broader structure was needed. We live in a time when ministries relating to demonic deliverance are rapidly increasing in the USA and in other parts of the world. Because ARDM was designed to build accountability through personal relationships, the size of the group had been limited to 25, and the meetings were conducted in a roundtable format. However, each of the ARDM members were acquainted with many other deliverance ministers whom they regarded as peers, but who could not become a part of ARDM because of size limitations.

Consequently, ARDM members agreed to expand the organization from a roundtable to a professional society. The name International Society of Deliverance Ministers (ISDM) was chosen. ISDM is not limited by size, and therefore it is able to serve any number of deliverance ministers who perceive value in associating with peers for the purpose of building relationships, learning from one another and expanding mutual integrity.

Presently ISDM is under the leadership and direction of Bill Sudduth founder of Righteous Acts Ministries, Inc. (RAM) in Stephens City, VA. Bill's vision for ISDM is to recognize and network deliverance ministers nationally and internationally. He also wants to restore a level of credibility to the ministry of deliverance by providing continuing education and peer level accountability for deliverance ministers. His goal is to see the ministry of deliverance and inner healing back in mainstream Christianity where it belongs. Bill ministers deliverance and inner healing on a daily basis and has ministered to thousands of people in both individual and group settings.

In January of 2015, Ernie and Silvia Sauve were appointed as Hispanic Ambassadors of ISDM. Our vision, in addition to the general vision of ISDM is to serve the Hispanic churches in the United States and Spanish speaking countries with training conferences and seminars. We invite you to learn more about becoming connected with like-minded deliverance and inner healing ministers by contacting us at:

http://daystream.org
http://liberacionenjesus.com
http://www.isdmministers.org/espanol
email: ernie@daystream.org
Twitter: @Ernie_SauveJr

Appendix 5

Special note from the Author

- Has the reading of this material impacted your life?
- Do you think your thoughts have changed after reading this book?
- Has it built you up?

If the answer is "YES" to any of the previous questions, I invite you to help others to be blessed as well.

Will you share about this book with your circle of friends, family and brothers and sisters in the faith? Here are some simple ideas to help you share: first, make a list of 10 people you know and want to tell them about this book. Think about your friends at church, your pastor, church leaders and other churches you know, even family members. I am sure they know somebody who is going through difficult situations without knowing that enemy of our soul is causing those situations. Most likely those people have many fears and insecurities and this book will help.

With the list in your hand,

1. Call them right now and tell them how this book: "Be more than a Conqueror" has impacted your life.

2. Go to Amazon.com and order a few to give to your loved ones as a gift of love.
3. On your Facebook or social media outlets, put the name of the book and the link on Amazon so that your friends can get it directly.
4. Send them a text or email with my email address: Silvia@daystream.com so they can order their book, I will gladly attend their request.

Did you know that when you help, then you also get help? It is the principle of sowing and reaping: you sow help; therefore, you will reap help and somebody will help you when you need it.

> *"Do not be deceived, God is not mocked; for whatever a man sows, that he will also reap."* Galatians 6: 7

> *"And let us not grow weary while doing good, for in due season we shall reap if we do not lose heart. Therefore, as we have opportunity, let us do good to all, especially to those who are of the household of faith."* Galatians 6: 9-10

Thank you for helping others, you are very special!

LIST OF PEOPLE YOU WILL HELP

1. _____

2. _____

3. _____

4. _____

5. _____

6. _____

7. _____

8. _____

9. _____

10. _____

NOTES